Kauai
...in my heart

...in my heart

HARRY T. YAMANAKA

Edited by Pamela Varma Brown

Write Path, LLC
Kapaa, Kauai, Hawaii

Write Path, LLC
Kapaa, Kauai, Hawaii

Copyright 2015 by Harry T. Yamanaka

Cover design: Aaron Yadao, Ink Spot Printing, Kauai, Hawaii
Book interior: Write Path, LLC
Title font: Fugu designed by Neil Summerour
Text font: Minion Pro

Cover photo:
Harry Yamanaka with one of the two bicycles
his family restored after someone else discarded them, complete with a Sears Roebuck seat cover, circa 1944.
The two bikes were the family's
only modes of transportation other than walking.

First Printing: July 2015

ISBN: 978-0-9856983-6-2 (Paperback)
ISBN: 978-0-9856983-7-9 (ebook)
Library of Congress Control Number: 2015944535

To my family

Acknowledgments

First of all, I thank my parents, who were both courageous enough to come from Japan to start new lives on the small Hawaiian island of Kauai in the early 1900s. They laid the groundwork for my siblings and me to have lives far beyond anything they might have imagined for us.

I thank my late wife, Jean, for tolerating my many hours of story-writing as I recalled my boyhood adventures. I miss you and our life together.

Thank you to my editor, Pamela Varma Brown, for her time editing my stories and placing them into this little volume, and to her proofreaders Viviane Stein, Karen McInnis and Lincoln Gill.

I grew up with Japanese being spoken by both my parents in our home, while primarily being surrounded by Hawaiians and Filipinos, who were our neighbors and my father's co-workers. My childhood was a bit of a blend of all three cultures, so you will notice in the stories that follow, a smattering of words from all of those languages, as that is how we spoke as children, and how many of us still speak as adults in Hawaii. English translations are in parentheses so you will be able to follow along.

I hope you enjoy reading about the fun I had growing up on the island of Kauai, and that these stories leave Kauai in your heart, too.

Aloha,

Harry Yamanaka
July 2015

Table of Contents

Kauai

...in my heart

Chapter 1
From Japan to Hawaii, 1907

My father, Kichijiro Yamanaka, bowed low and gently grasped his mother's hands.

"Only three years and I will be back," he whispered.

His mother (my grandmother) bowed slightly with her palms resting on her thighs and looked deeply into the eyes of her 17-year-old son.

"Work hard. Endure. Keep this charm," she said, handing him a small omamori (good luck) pouch that he gently put in his pocket. "I will see you in three years."

My grandfather stood a few paces behind, nervously glancing at the commotion on the busy Yokohama docks: Japanese men, women and children bustling around them; steamships lining the piers while men loaded and unloaded cargo; everyone attired in their best dark-colored kimonos.

As people walked the gangplank onto the stately steamship, the vessel swayed and creaked as passengers bound for Hawaii got on board. The large ship sounded its horn, signaling it was time for all passengers be aboard and all others to disembark.

"I'll return with a lot of money and pay the taxes my parents owe to the Japanese government," my father thought to himself. "Then my parents can live peacefully on their land."

But as the ship gently rolled in the tides of Tokyo Bay, Kichijiro's parents had an ominous feeling that this would be the last time they would see their Number Two son.

$$\approx \approx \approx$$

Father knew that longstanding Japanese tradition dictated that his older brother would inherit anything the family owned, and also its debts. My grandfather owed land taxes to the Japanese government that were long overdue, meaning that my father, as the second-born son, would be left with nothing.

So when my father was recruited as part of a large group of Japanese laborers sent to Hawaii in 1907 to work for the sugar plantations, he welcomed the opportunity. It was the middle of a wave of Japanese immigration that, by the turn of the century, saw 61,000 Japanese nationals move to Hawaii. Kanyaku Imin, the official contract labor agreement between Hawaii and the Japanese government, had ended 13 years earlier and formal indentured contracts were a thing of the past. However, the tacit understanding remained that Japanese laborers were expected to work in Hawaii for a contract period of three years or more.

In a way, my grandfather was happy to see his son

move on, as he understood the financial ramifications of their family's predicament. But to seek adventure in Japan was one thing. Going to a strange land like Hawaii was more than what he liked. But it was only to be for three years, so he had given his son his blessing.

≈ ≈ ≈

The steam clipper crossed the 3,300 nautical miles from Yokohama to the Hawaiian island of Oahu at full speed, its smokestack belching black smoke and the sails spread taut from the power of the wind. After two weeks at sea, Oahu's Koolau Mountains became visible on the horizon, rising 3,100 feet above the ocean's surface.

As the sun warmed their faces, Father joined the passengers lining the deck to get their first glimpse of Hawaii. A long, low mountain range in the center of the island ran lengthwise, a green slope all the way to the ocean. A heavy raincloud covered the highest peak; a huge double rainbow united the sky, the mountains and the sea. Magnificent!

Exiting the ship, my father joined the 900 other passengers who were lined up to walk on a wooden bridge to Quarantine Island (now known as Sand Island) at the entrance to Honolulu Harbor, where they were to be quarantined for two weeks before moving on to their final destinations.

Each immigrant received a number written on a piece of cardboard that they were required to hang around their neck. The numbers indicated which sugar plantation they were assigned to and also helped immigration authorities, who were somewhat overwhelmed by the homogeneity of the Japanese, to identify them. My father's number was somewhere in the thousands.

"Put your hand up when I say your name," shouted an immigration official, whose mangled pronunciation of Japanese names was difficult for the new immigrants to understand.

"Abe." No hands went up.

"Yama." No hands. "Yama! Yama!" Still no response, but a kimono-clad young man fidgeted as if that was his name.

"You, Yama?" the official asked.

My father pointed at himself and said, "Yamanaka."

"From Wakayama?"

"Hai *(Yes),*" my father said, nodding his head. "Ya-manaka."

Immigration officials who recorded the names at the quarantine station had no idea about the sacredness of Japanese names. They wrote them according to how the names sounded and abbreviated the ones they could not understand. Many Japanese kept their "new" names, while others corrected their names once they arrived on the plantations and reported for work.

After their quarantine period was over, Father and other men boarded the steamship S.S. Kinau bound for the island of Kauai. They arrived at Nawiliwili Harbor the next day. In the confusion at Nawiliwili, the Kipu Sugar Plantation escort accepted my father as an employee, although he had not been assigned to any specific plantation.

He was taken to a dormitory for single men where

sleeping spaces measured only 10 by 12 feet. Each man had to take a bath before sleeping and no talking was allowed; sleep was the only activity permitted. No one disputed this order, because working, eating and sleeping was the routine to which all of the men in the dormitory adhered.

For several months, Father worked long days in the sugar cane fields, returning to his 120-square-foot space each evening. He began to wonder what life was all about.

My father, Kichijiro Yamanaka, in 1915 at Kipu

In one of these moments of uncertainty, he met a Hawaiian man who had come to Lihue (two miles east of Kipu) from the very remote Kalalau Valley on the north shore of the island, to purchase supplies. My father was starving and the stranger offered him piping hot laulau, meat or fish wrapped in ti or banana leaves and steamed, from a nearby vendor. He invited Father to join him living in Kalalau Valley, a completely undeveloped part of the island, where they would live off the land.

My father was ready for some adventure and gladly accepted the stranger's offer. Together, one on a mule, the other on a horse, they rode 10 hours to the trailhead, then hiked 11 miles into Kalalau Valley. Father spoke only Japanese and the man spoke only Hawaiian, but by communicating with hand gestures and facial expressions, they felt like long-lost buddies reunited by the time they reached the valley. Within a year of living in Kalalau Valley, Father was fluent in the Hawaiian language.

While in Japan, Father had learned how to farm, and he was an expert fisherman. Hawaiians in the valley taught him how to plant taro, and he showed his new friends the process of rice-making.

He also managed to divert some of the rice grains to make a drink called sake, Japanese rice wine. The locals already were making a drink called okolehao, an alcoholic drink from the root of the ti plant, but another variety was welcomed by the Hawaiians.

Father lived the commune life in Kalalau for seven years. Once he turned 26 years old, he knew from his Japanese upbringing that it was time to begin his family life.

He made his way back to Kipu Sugar Plantation,

where he was welcomed back with open arms by the plantation owner, William Hyde Rice. This turned out to be a blessing for me, because my years growing up in Kipu are some of the most special times of my life.

Chapter 2
Mother

My mother, Haruno Hiraoka, was born in Heigun, Japan, an island of about 1,000 people, that made the village of Kipu seem large. When she was 2 years old, her parents left Japan to work on Kauai, leaving Haruno to grow up in the homes of various relatives. Her longest stay was with her uncle who was mute. She never had a life of formal schooling. She could not read or write in Japanese nor in English. She could, however, write her name in Katakana, a form of Japanese phonetic writing. She grew up strong, independent and open to adventure.

When Mother's parents sent for her to join them in Hawaii, she was 16 years old and hardly knew them. She was reluctant to remove herself from the only life she had known to live with people who were, in essence, strangers to her. Yet she made the journey to Kauai, where her parents were in the midst of successive three-year contracts for the Lihue Sugar Plantation.

Once on Kauai she spent most of her time doing

domestic chores, looking after her three brothers and a younger sister while her parents labored long hours on the plantation. My grandmother took in laundry work for some men working at the plantation and Mother was responsible for washing and ironing those clothes.

When Mother was 16, her parents chose a distant cousin in Heigun, Japan, for her to marry. Mother was not overly enthusiastic over that matrimonial possibility and balked at the marriage. She had known the young man from her years in Japan and found him boring.

And in the meantime, she had met a fascinating and handsome Japanese man on Kauai.

Chapter 3
My Parents Fall in Love

*A*s was customary for Japanese men working in Hawaii in those days, my father's parents sought to find him a wife, a woman in Japan via a picture-bride arrangement. A marriage broker had sent photos of a chosen candidate two times, but both failed to meet Father's approval. Living and working abroad on his own, he had a developed a freelance lifestyle. It seemed that the choice of a mate was a personal one that only he could do for himself.

On his days off from working on Kipu Plantation, my father often ran errands in Lihue, and as fate would have it, one day he spotted Haruno Hiraoka, the woman who was to become my mother. Soon Father found himself riding the sugar cane delivery train from Kipu to Lihue every Sunday to court this quiet yet spirited young lady.

Father was intrigued. Haruno seemed like a very simple woman, but she was also strong, healthy, nice to look at, young and chose to do things her own way. Likewise, Mother found this man's confidence appealed to her own self-sufficient nature that she had cultivated during her years living an ocean away from her parents. It was a good match.

But my mother's parents disliked this man from Kipu. He was tall, handsome, 11 years her senior, and talkative, which was quite out of character for a Japanese man. They knew that he was on his second work agreement with Kipu Plantation, seemed unable to save any money and certainly could not afford to return to Japan. "This won't do," they said.

Mother's parents had scrimped and saved for their journey back to Japan. After fulfilling both of their three-year contracts for Lihue Sugar Plantation, they were ready to return to Heigun. The plan was for the entire family to come with them, including their daughter Haruno.

But several days before the family's departure date, my mother disappeared. A frantic search for her ensued in both Lihue and Kipu. My father, coincidentally, was missing from work at the same time.

In a quandary, Mother's parents left for Japan without her. They had four other children to look after and could not divert much effort to look for this dissenting daughter. They had worked too hard and too long to earn the money to pay for their return voyage to forfeit it. They knew Haruno was with my father, and although they were not overjoyed at this, they somehow knew that she was safe.

The lovers hid out in an abandoned shack by Oba Pond above the Huleia Valley on Kipu Plantation land. Mr. Rice, the owner of Kipu Plantation, discouraged any searches on his property. With a wink of his eye, he provided assurance to my father that their secret was safe with him.

After Mother's family left for Japan, my parents trekked to Koloa on the south shore of Kauai — an arduous journey in those days — to make their life official as a married couple. They chose this route rather than being pledged together by the Buddhist minister, as was Japanese tradition, because they knew the Buddhist minister had likely heard about my mother's disappearance and that could have led to complications.

Life for this young couple in the little shack was primitive. One of the sugar plantation's irrigation ditches meandered nearby. The nearest neighbor and plantation headquarters were each one mile away and the nearest general store, Hamano Store, was two miles away — all far in an era when most people lived within very short walking distance from everything they needed. Transportation as we know it today was many years away from being developed.

Fortunately Father was a part-time luna (supervisor) for the plantation and as such was allowed to keep a mule. The beast became indispensable for helping bring home 100-pound bags of rice from Hamano Store, my father's catches of fresh-water fish, normally mullet, that he caught in Huleia River, and the huge Samoan crabs that he caught with his crab nets.

In quick succession, my parents had four children and the grass shack became unsuitable for the growing family. Eventually, a four-bedroom house was made available at Stable Camp, one of the nearby "camps" or settlements of single-wall construction wooden homes provided by the sugar plantation to its employees. Once my family moved to the new quarters, many more children were born.

I was born the ninth of my parents' 13 children. I was the youngest son.

Before me, there was my sister Hanae, later called Juliet, my brother Yoshio (renamed Sam as a young man when a few vendors to his plumbing supply business found that name easier), sister Tetsuko (Gladys), sister Harue (Margie), brother Goro, sister Satsuki (Esther), brother Muneto (Paul) and brother Kiyoshi (William). After me were my sisters Kikue (Kitt), Jisae (Edith), Tonie (Doris) and Jeanne.

It is rumored by other family members that I was my mother's pet. Anyone who gave me lickins (spankings) was subject to Mother's wrath. That was something to contend with because Mother was a very large woman and could tussle with the best of them. As a result, I developed a laissez-faire personality and seldom did any of my homework.

Opposite:
My mother and father, Haruno and Kichijiro Yamanaka,
with my oldest siblings, Yoshio, later called Sam, on my
mother's lap, and Hanae, who was later called Juliet.

Chapter 4
Growing Up On Kauai

I can still see the old plantation house in Rice Camp where our family of 15 lived. It was a typical wooden, single-walled construction house that was made available to all plantation field workers with four bedrooms and one living room. The kitchen was separate, adjoined by a walkway. We all fit in the house somehow. We doubled up, slept on the floor. As a child I didn't think about it much because I didn't know any better.

Our neighbors on one side were Filipino bachelors who worked long hours and tended to their roosters tethered in the yard. Our neighbors on the other side were the Kagawas. I remember clearly Jimmy, one of the Kagawa sons, and his irritating whistle to signal the kids in our household to keep quiet.

The area around the plantation camp was full of peacocks, roosters and hens. No one was allowed to catch them, and Kauai was free of mongoose, a natural predator, so the birds were everywhere. They slept in trees and woke up early to announce their delight at the new day.

The crowing and cawing were incessantly present in the early morning hours. Did you ever hear the loud scream from a peacock or guinea hen in the darkness of early morning? It did not bother me, but I am sure it would not be the same for someone who has never experienced this.

I painted this picture of a typical Kauai sugar plantation camp house from images that permanently reside in my mind and heart.

My father was a trackman tending the plantation's railroad tracks. He also served as a middleman for the employees to talk about their problems and grievances to the management. He earned about $35 a month and that was more than many other men.

Our life revolved around the small sphere of the plantation, Rice Camp, local fishing spots, Hamano Store, Seki Camp and Stable Camp, which were other plantation camps nearby. We walked everywhere or we rode one of the two bicycles our family repaired and rebuilt, claimed after someone had thrown them away. When I visited Rice Camp several years after moving away, I jogged the three miles from Hamano Store to the main highway. I was surprised that this distance was such a short run, and yet at that time no one searched out this greater world.

When I was growing up, you walked to get anywhere or rode a bicycle if you had one. No one had a car except two families who spent most of their time polishing their cars instead of driving them around. No one else could afford such luxuries. If we were walking when a car came by, they almost always stopped to give you a ride. Back then, it was a pleasure to ride in a car.

We shopped for necessities at Hamano Store, owned by a Chinese couple and managed by the husband. He usually gave you a piece of candy or ice cream if you made the trip to his store. Back then it was a very welcome item and everyone was thrilled to get it. When he didn't want to go to the freezer to get an ice cream, he would give you a soda, and it was a joy to receive.

There was only one policeman in the area. His presence got everyone's attention. Actually there was no need for police work because most of the problems were handled internally and most were non-violent. None of the homes had keys to the door. Break-ins were non-existent. Besides, what was there to steal?

Chapter 5
No One Starved

I have often wondered how my mother raised 13 children in this "camp" or village at the Kipu Sugar Plantation. Imagine 13 kids to feed, clothe and discipline, among other problems. By any standard, that is a very large family to feed. But how did my mother do this on the meager $35 paycheck that my father brought home? And with his generous consumption of sake (Japanese rice wine), which took a lot of money to perpetuate, it was a challenge. She also had no electric stove, no refrigeration, no washing machine, no heater and just about no other conveniences.

Our family had three large vegetable gardens, supervised by Mother. I earned pocket money by selling burdock, a plant much in demand by Japanese families for use of the crunchy root called gobo in nishime, a traditional Japanese stew made with root vegetables. Gobo is difficult to grow because the dirt has to be softened to about two feet from the top to provide a good media for growing long and tender roots. My father allowed me to keep the money from selling gobo to meet my various expenses. My bank was a small drawer where I kept loose change. In those days it was not wise to hold money in your pockets because of the bullies who took whatever you had.

With the vegetables grown in the three gardens, with at least two pigs at any given time (we shared the pork when the pigs were slaughtered), with lots of chickens in the pens, with the hillside and mountain providing lots of local fruits, with wild pigs in the mountains, with fish from the river and reservoirs, with an array of leftover products from the cattle that were slaughtered each week, no one starved.

We boiled the big and wild Portuguese taro that grew in abundance near the ditches. Tofu was made by the Kodama family and sold at a very reasonable price. An uncle in Lihue occasionally sent three-day-old bread for us and we also collected garbage from the nearby families. A neighbor regularly gave us tripe from the cattle that the plantation slaughtered weekly.

To satisfy one's sweet tooth, we children walked along the train tracks that ran through the plantation and picked up stalks of fallen sugar cane. We sliced off the skin with a pocketknife and chewed the pulp to get to the sweet sugar. We also made arrows of the long leaves with our knives, whipping the leaves into the air and watching the arrows fly to distant spots.

In those days, a penny went a long way. For instance, a loaf of unsliced bread cost five cents. School lunch cost five cents also. Schools did not offer free lunches for economically challenged families. Had there been such support, my family would have been highly qualified for that program.

Still, Mother had to manipulate her situation like a wizard to have only two of my siblings, Marge and Paul, temporarily taken away by a roving nurse to be treated for malnutrition at the public health center in the Samuel Mahelona Memorial Hospital on the east side of the island.

To this day, I am baffled as to how my mother fed us as well as she did. I really don't know. However, I do know there was food on the stove at all times for everyone. Our favorites were corned beef and cabbage, tripe stew, dry sausage and rice. To this day, I never complain about the food that is served. Everything is palatable. These days my favorite fast food meal is from a nearby restaurant that makes excellent tripe stew. The taste is comparable to my mother's preparation.

And fortunately the plantation provided a house, water, medical service, firewood and electricity, and had a crew of carpenters who fixed whatever broke in our home.

Like Exquisite Chicken

It seemed that everyone in the family had a role to play in these times of plantation survival. I helped by catching frogs. Frogs are very good eating, something like exquisite chicken. Cleaning frogs was easy. Just cut the head off, rip the skin from the neck down and take out the guts.

Frogs were plentiful in ditches. On some frog-catching expeditions with a neighbor, I caught a half bag or more. One day when visiting Hanalei with a friend, I learned that frogs were even more abundant and easier to catch in the taro fields on the island's north shore. We walked along the earthen dikes between the taro patches and instead of spearing them, my friend just put one leg in the water and caught them at the throat by jamming them against the dirt banks. I was the bag boy and in the end the gunny sack was almost full of live frogs. It got so heavy I had to say, "Enough!" My friend chopped off the legs from the trunk section and told me he sent them to a restaurant in Honolulu and made an excellent profit.

As an adult, I ordered frog legs in Paris, but the French always add a dressing to go with it. I prefer them with shoyu (soy) sauce.

The Biggest Samoan Crab

Once a week my older brother Sam paddled his home-made canoe to the dense mangrove growth in the Huleia River to catch Samoan crabs. More than once Sam had bagged a sack full of those crabs using a bait of bacalao (cod), an item that was sold relatively cheaply those days at the Hamano Store.

On this day, Sam felt the weight of something heavy in his net. He thought it was piece of snagged log, but upon bagging it, he discovered that it was a 13½ pound Samoan crab. He could hardly believe that such a huge monster existed in the muddy waters of the Huleia River. The crabs he had caught in the past were much smaller.

When Sam got home, he asked me to go with him to sell the crabs to the Filipino men in town. Even though I was young, riding shotgun was very exciting to me.

While we were riding along, Sam told me that one of the crabs he caught that day was very large. In my curiosity, I stuck my hand into the bag. Immediately the monster crab grabbed my hand in its powerful claw and would not let go. I hurriedly pulled my hand out of the bag — with the claw and crab attached — and began screaming bloody murder.

Sam got his oar and hit the crustacean, dislodging the crab, but its claw remained attached to my hand, gripping my fingers. I continued screaming in pain while Sam drove home. Once we got inside the house, he got a pot of water boiling, then dipped the claw into the water, careful to save my fingers from the heat. That did the trick: the claw muscle relaxed, and I got my hand back.

Fortunately for our household, the rest of the huge crab was not salable with its detached claw. We had a nice dinner with that crab as the centerpiece. The amount of meat was enormous and it provided a full meal for the Yamanaka clan, a blessing for our plantation family of 15.

≈ ≈ ≈

As an adult, I learned the art of taxidermy. I recently mounted a large Samoan crab that was snagged in the Wailoa Pond in the city of Hilo on the Big Island of Hawaii, where I now live. It was nowhere near the size of the one Sam caught many years ago, but it was rather large compared to the size we normally see today. I asked the owner if he would prefer to eat it. He said, no, that it was the biggest crab he ever caught and he wanted to hang it on his trophy wall. I think that is wise because a fisherman's tale is very suspect today.

I checked at a market in Hilo that sells exotic merchandise, but was told they do not carry Samoan crab. I guess that in order to satisfy my longing for that special crab flavor, I must now try my luck the old way at the Huleia River on Kauai. I wonder if there are some big ones still lurking on the bottom of that river.

When I return to Kauai each summer to visit, I gaze into Huleia Valley and nostalgia strikes me. My palate tells me that Samoan crabs still dwell in the muddy river bottom. They are smaller in size than when we were children, but a skillful fisherman can catch a few. And I know how to handle a claw that has latched onto my fingers: simply take it home, boil it, then eat it.

Johnny Appleseed of Kipu

I have often thought of my father as the Johnny Appleseed of Kipu. Like the legendary man who wandered across the country in the late 1700s and early 1800s planting apple trees, my father planted seeds for all kinds of plants as he walked to and from work, to help feed our large family. His mantra was, "Only grow what you can eat."

What I remember most was the little sack of seeds he carried in his bento bag (lunch bag). He would stop on his way to the sugar cane fields to plant squash, pumpkin and cucumber along the irrigation ditches. On days when I played hooky from school, I tagged along to dig holes and clear the grass wherever he pointed so he could plant seeds.

In a few months these seeds would grow and Father would direct us children to harvest the crops. It was fun walking through the tall buffalo grass and wild honohono orchids looking for mature fruits.

In those days, no one would take what belonged to another person, so fruits and vegetables remained in plain view, wherever my father had planted them. As a matter of fact, I never realized that a house should be locked until I went to college in Wisconsin, where we didn't know our neighbors. In Kipu you knew your neighbors so well that you even knew every detail of what they ate for dinner. Thievery was not a problem in Kipu.

I learned to appreciate all the fruit trees in our neighborhood and scattered around in the nearby mountains and valleys. There was wi apple (pronounced "vee" apple), mountain apple, star apple, guava, ulu (breadfruit), mango, coconut and lots of orange trees. Anyone could pick these wild fruits.

Mango trees were everywhere when I was growing up in Kipu. One mango tree gave enough fruit for many children — and chickens loved to peck at ripe mangoes that had fallen to the ground.

My favorite way to eat mangoes is when they are half-ripe and still green, especially when seasoned with shoyu and salt, or with sugar. As children, we knew it was wise to carry a small bottle of shoyu (soy sauce) and a pocket-knife to feast on wild mangoes — delicious and excellent for lunch!

To this day, I wonder who planted all those fruit trees because when I was a young boy, they were already quite large, yet Kipu was largely undeveloped and has always been sparsely populated ever since I can remember. Maybe they were planted by Native Hawaiians long before I was born, or by Polynesian voyagers, since a number of the varieties are usually found in Tahiti. But as a child, I just picked the ripe fruits and didn't worry about their origin.

The wi apple, also known as ambarella fruit, grew along the ditches near pig pens. I enjoyed picking up the apples that had fallen to the ground, filling a bucket with them and feeding the pigs. The pigs loved this and crunched the apples easily, whereas we humans had to struggle to get the meat of the fruit away from the nasty spikes growing from the pit.

Mountain apples, also known as Malay apples, are tiny, red pear-shaped apples that grew along the mountainsides. As children, we fashioned holders from leaves of Hawaiian ti plants, filled our homemade baskets full of mountain apples and brought them home to eat.

The only ulu (breadfruit) tree I saw as a boy grew in the yard of an angry person. When the heavy fruits dropped from the tree to the grass, they left a mess. It did not look very palatable and as a child, I thought it befit only pigs. As I grew older, I learned that ulu is a staple in many countries, though I still harbor the image of it as pig food.

My brother, Goro, was an expert maker of bamboo fishing poles that had a whip excellent for setting the hook on a fish. He started with a mature, long, sturdy stalk of bamboo, then built a small fire and passed the nodes of the bamboo over the heat. The bamboo softened and became pliable. As sap oozed onto the surface, he wiped the oily beads with a rag. In a few minutes, an original green bamboo pole would be finished and leaned against a wall to dry for about two weeks.

As boys, we fished at reservoirs stocked with black bass called Charlie Fish. One reservoir, called Turning, had an abundance of fish but an oft-told story about the ghost of Felix scared a lot of us away. During my brothers' long walks to and from Huleia Valley to the east of Rice Camp, they brought back fish including papio, mullet, gobi and aholehole, supplementing the small amount of meat our family could get.

As I recall my years growing up in Kipu, I find that we were a very fortunate family since the land provided so much for us. Money was always a problem for my parents but the land provided so much to us that no one starved in Kipu.

And even more fortunately, the Hamano Store proprietor let us continue to charge food on our account and although our balance continued to grow, our account was never closed.

Chapter 6
Hamano Store

*M*r. Hamano was a short, balding man with a pencil stuck over his right ear, forever perched on his high stool in his office at the back of the store. I never saw him without that pencil. Years later, whenever I visit the site where the Hamano Store once stood, I can see the store and the tiny gas station in my imagination and I also see Mr. Hamano sitting on his stool, cranking his calculator, tabulating business at the end of the day and every morning as each day began.

As the only store in our area, situated on a corner where east meets west and north meets south, where a mile-long road lined with towering Norfolk pine trees greets the pohaku (stone) monument of Mr. Rice that my father carved, the Hamano Store became a landmark. "I'll meet you at Hamano Store" was a common refrain.

Mr. Hamano was alert and ever-cognizant of anyone entering his store, his pointer dog responding to anyone with a recognizable cadence of its footsteps. Mr. Hamano would look up and come out to attend to a customer or a deliveryman whenever his assistant or wife were not around.

Mr. Hamano always had a yard boy and a maid for his house. Many boys filled the yard boy position and my brother, William, was his most reliable. I replaced William when my brother went to work for Grove Farm Company during the summer months. A person by the name of Tony also worked there, and my sisters, Kitt and Juliet, and a few of the Kodama girls worked as maids. Kitt received a meager five cents to work there after school washing dishes, cleaning the kitchen and the toilet, and was paid sometimes by the month at $2. She worked there for five years, each day after school. The pay was so paltry that our sister, Edith, refused to replace her when Kitt left the job.

We were all young when we worked there. Kitt was 10 years old when she started on the job. I was 11 when I worked as a yard boy. William drove the delivery truck before he had a driver's license.

≈ ≈ ≈

I don't think Mr. Hamano liked me much. In those lean years, if you did a good job for him, he rewarded you with a soda, pastry or a candy bar. Otherwise an oral evaluation was given to your parents — and my report from him was that I was a lazy boy. As you can imagine, I never received a free dole. My father never reprimanded me about my work habits, but I know he was relieved when my brother returned to work at the store after his summer working for Grove Farm. My parents wanted to stay on Mr. Hamano's good side.

Visions of the Hamano Store still linger in my mind. I painted this painting from my memories of our childhood store.

I must indicate that Mr. Hamano was an astute businessman and had a unique system. No cash was collected at the time of a transaction; the total was added onto your running balance. Back then, a loaf of bread cost about five cents, a bag of rice cost about $2. In the year 1942, the Yamanaka family total owed to the Hamano Store was

$1,400. When looking at the rate of inflation, that would have amounted to about $20,000 to $30,000 in today's dollars. You can see how that became a problem for us.

Mr. Hamano charged a bit more for some clients in comparison to other families. No one knew how he accounted for these discrepancies, but my parents were happy that they could continue to charge without paying their balance in full. Eventually, if there was nonpayment, a bill collector would surely knock on your door and you would lose your credit rating or you would not be allowed on the premises. I suppose when Mr. Hamano charged a bit more for some, it is similar to what we know as a service or interest charge today.

≈ ≈ ≈

In a typical Japanese family, the eldest son assumes the family's burdens if necessary. It was that way with the Yamanaka family. My oldest brother, Sam, was expected to inherit the life problems of our family and he bore the brunt of our family malaise.

I had a telephone conversation with Sam once we were adults and learned that the ambivalent feelings I had as a child about Mr. Hamano were totally wrong.

Sam left school at the end of the eighth grade to work at the Kipu Sugar Plantation to help with our family's financial situation. There were many children in the family and our father was one of those who favored a paternalistic drinking life. Father was very responsible in other ways, but his meager paycheck was not enough to feed the family, especially because his needs included the cost of sake and ingredients for his home brew.

Before Sam left Kauai for the island of Oahu in search of more lucrative jobs in Honolulu, he reached an agreement with Mr. Hamano that Mother would be allowed to continue charging on her account and that Sam would pay it off from his earnings.

But when World War II began, getting work in Honolulu became difficult. The Japanese were discriminated against in the Naval shipyards, even Japanese Americans who were born in Hawaii.

But Sam found other work opportunities. He started with jobs as a bus driver for the Honolulu Rapid Transit and as a dishwasher for a restaurant. He sent Mr. Hamano about $25 each month to pay off the balance. It took some time, but Sam persevered and the Hamano bill was eventually paid in full.

But World War II had a disastrous consequence for Mr. Hamano. He was deemed to be a threat to the security of our nation by the United States government, one of 120,000 people of Japanese ethnicity in the U.S. who were torn from their homes and businesses without warning, solely because of their ethnicity, and imprisoned in internment camps across the country.

But even without Mr. Hamano, life had to continue and Hamano Store still fulfilled the needs of the Kipu people. Mrs. Hamano continued as the elementary teacher at the Huleia Grammar School; a man named Mr. Nishimura came to manage the store; and Mr. Sadamitsu, the store's traveling salesman, continued his responsibilities.

By the time Mr. Hamano was released from the internment camps, returned to Kauai and resumed his place at the Hamano Store, the demographics of the neighborhood had changed a lot. Kipu Sugar Plantation had given up on sugar cane and the owner went into the ranching business. Some employees went to work on the Grove Farm sugar plantation and many — including the older Yamanaka family members — moved to Honolulu for work. The Huleia Grammar School was no longer across the road from Hamano Store and only a few families remained in Stable Camp. A few years later Mr. Sadamitsu left to start his own store in the former Yoneji Store location in Lihue. He already had Lihue clientele from his work with Hamano Store, cutting further into Mr. Hamano's declining customer base.

Then, the final coupe de grace happened. Hurricane Iwa swept over Kauai in 1982, destroyed Mr. Hamano's home and the store became a shambles. Fortunately, the Hamanos had a second home in the town of Kilauea on the north shore of Kauai. They left Kipu to live there and later moved to Honolulu, where Mrs. Hamano was originally from. In 1992, Hurricane Iniki blew through Kauai, knocking over some Norfolk pine trees and devastating what was left of the Hamano Store building.

Even though my youthful experiences left me with a negative feeling about Mr. Hamano, as I see it now, he was a savior for the families of Kipu. Where would we have been if there was no kindness in this man? He ran the Hamano Store in service for the community. He was taken away for a few years to be confined in an internment camp, then returned to Kipu after being jailed and tried to put the pieces of his life back in order, in spite of all the ensuing problems. Then a hurricane destroyed what he tried to do. His only claim to a seeming wealth was a modest home in the town of Kilauea.

My memories of Hamano Store and of our small community are captured in this painting. I compressed three elements that were on the corner of the road to make a better composition: I moved the Haupu Mountain range behind the store; the pohaku (stone monument) was eased over to the left; and a lone trunk of a Norfolk pine was painted on the right border to represent mile-long Puhi Road that was lined with towering pine trees. Two men sitting on the bench in the early morning hours are waiting to be picked up for work. The lights in the windows indicate that someone is inside working. The delivery-man from Tip Top Bakery arrives very early to drop off bread and pastries. The pointer dog, eagerly tapping the door from the inside, is awaiting his pastry treat that the delivery man gives him every day at the Hamano Store.

≈ ≈ ≈

As I visit the site today, the Norfolk pines on the mile-long road leading into Kipu still stand as statues. A wagon full of tourists comes chugging up the dirt road, paying customers of a Kipu trail-riding company that takes them on a tour of ranch grounds from the stable to the foothills of the Haupu range, to the lookout from Field 11 where sugar cane once grew, over the Menehune Fish Pond on the rim of the Huleia Valley, to the former grounds of the Japanese language school and the Hamano Store.

But the Hamano house and the Hamano Store are both gone now; a cattle fence is the only reminder that a bustling store that served our community once stood here. I will forever cherish memories of the Hamano Store.

Chapter 7
My First Fishing Canoe

This story is written from the perspective of my 8-year-old self in 1940, when I enjoyed fishing at Kuraya Pond on Kauai. Today, the Kuraya house that was near the pond no longer exists and the pond is now a watering hole for the cattle on Kipu Ranch.

Last week my friend and I sneaked over to the Kajiwara bamboo farm to cut a long bamboo stalk to make a fishing pole. On the road to the bamboo farm, we also cut a few bamboo shoots, called takenoko, because Mother always likes to cook them. It is nice to have a new, shiny long pole and a pocketknife.

We used to be very successful hooking a full load of fish, but we think the fish are wiser now and have moved into the deeper water. We are hoping that a longer pole will whip the bait further into the deep water of Kuraya Pond so we can catch more black bass that we call "Charlie Fish."

On our return to our rambling plantation house boxed in by Norfolk pine trees, my friend walks in front of me because I am carrying the long pole on my shoulders. It is a bit dangerous to walk last in line in the waning evening on plantation roads because wild animals and ghosts of the night could creep up from behind you.

When I get home, my big brother, Goro, builds a small fire in the front yard and passes the crooked joints of the bamboo pole over the fire to straighten it out. It is very uncomfortable to hold a crooked bamboo pole when fishing. Like magic from the heat of the fire, the green bamboo turns a bit yellowish. A good fishing pole is stylish. Only old people fish with poles that have a cut-off front end or poles that aren't shiny.

Goro eyeballs the pole from the bottom end and straightens each section out by bending it on his knee, a burlap bag protecting his leg from the still-hot bamboo. After he is satisfied that it is straight, he whisks the entire pole over the fire to get out all of the sap, wipes it clean with the burlap bag and holds the pole from the bottom end to inspect his work. He notices that the upper part of the pole veers to the right so he places that section over the fire again and straightens it out. He lowers the pole parallel to the ground and shakes the top end and declares that it is good.

"Here, I hope you like 'em and can catch some big ones," Goro says.

I grab the straight yellow pole and jiggle it to make sure it works for me. It whips and swooshes, the sounds of a very flexible bamboo fishing pole. I am already visualizing hooking on to a very hungry big bass. "T'anks, Goro," I say.

Now, my problem is how to get myself to the deeper waters of Kuraya Pond. I could float on a rubber tube, but then I would have to lug around my long pole and my bait, hooks, floaters and a stringer. I try to think of another way.

I remember the story of Huckleberry Finn that our third-grade teacher, Mrs. Hamano, read to us, and how Huck poled his way along the Mississippi River on a raft. I think Huck Finn is really stylish with a straw hat and coveralls. I wear coveralls, too. But Huck Finn's story is only a fairy tale. In real life, I could paddle my raft out with oars or by stroking with my hands, but all the noise I would make in the water would scare the fish away. There must be a better way.

Why not make a canoe like the ancient Indians and Hawaiians did? There were several problems with this idea. Surely I am not big enough to cut down a tree. I also do not have a large saw nor an axe, and besides, the luna (sugar plantation supervisor) would probably catch me and give me a good scolding.

Then I remember that a few years ago, I saw my older brother banging away at a discarded tin roof and he made a canoe of it. I could use a trunk of hau bush as the outrigger "arm" that would keep it upright while in the water; there are lots of hau trees growing over the river. I could make my paddle with a discarded piece of 1x4 lumber.

When my brother had his tin roof canoe, he paddled around in the Huleia River and caught a lot of Samoan crabs and sold them in the village. My visions are not that grandiose. I only want to get to the deep waters of the Kuraya Pond to catch fish for our family to eat.

I look under our house and come across a pile of tin roof sheets where my father stores them to replace leaky roof panels over his storage room. Most of the tin sheets are rusty and have large nail holes, but I find the best-looking one. With a large hammer from my father's tool chest, I pound the corrugated sections flat.

Normally, noise in a plantation village does not attract anyone's attention. At any given time during the day, people are hand-sawing logs and chopping them into smaller pieces; the blacksmith pounds horseshoes into shape on his anvil; the milkman clops along the street with his huge horses and a wagon; parents discipline kids; fighting cocks crow continuously in Filipinos' yards; and dogs bark from every household.

My mother, however, finds the sound of my banging alarming and stops washing clothes to see what is happening.

"Tora-chan nani deki masu, ka?" (What are you making?)

"I … am … making … a … canoe," I say between my pounding on the tin roof material.

"Doko de tsuka imasu ka?" (Where are you going to use this?)

"Kuraya Pondo. Sakana tsuru ni ikimasu." (Kuraya Pond. I am going fishing.)

Fortunately, my mother is satisfied that I am not doing any mischief. But, she ventures to ask me a question that I had never thought of:

"Fukai toko itala, abunai desho?" (Isn't it dangerous

for you to go in the deep water?)

"Never mind that. I must get to that bass," I grumble and continue with my hammering.

Much to my dismay, I really cannot swim more than 10 yards, as my mother knows. I know how to dog paddle, because the older kids like to harass the younger ones by throwing them into the deeper parts of Kuraya Pond, and we have to do something to stay afloat and keep our head above the water's surface. Dogs do that without instructions. But the dog paddle is slow and will only take me a short distance. The middle of Kuraya Pond is about 50 yards away from the shoreline and that requires a swimmer's stroke, such as the Australian crawl. But I don't want to think about that right now.

Eventually, I get the roof iron flattened out. I nail 2x4s on both ends, and the thing resembles a canoe. I get two hau tree stumps and lash them onto the 2x4s and saw the smaller 1x4 piece of lumber into the shape of a paddle. I am now ready for the big show.

My friend helps me carry the canoe on the half-mile trip through the sugarcane field roads to Kuraya Pond. We stumble along, hoping that the lunas will be busy chastising the cane field workers and not be riding their horses on these side roads. Fortunately, no one sees us and we arrive safely at the pond.

We throw the canoe into the water. With paddles in hand, we sit on the crosspieces. Immediately water begins leaking into the canoe through the small nail holes. It will be a total disaster for us if the canoe sinks in the middle of the pond.

We hurriedly pull the canoe back to shore, dump the

water out and hide it in the pond reeds. We run to the house and get a can of black tin tar that my father uses to patch the leaking roof. By the time we return, the canoe is dry enough to absorb the tar. We lavishly patch every hole and crevice and deem the canoe "seaworthy." We drag it into the water again and paddle a short distance to the deep side to test it out. It works perfectly.

We return home at 3 p.m. and decide to take the canoe out for a fishing excursion an hour later. We keep our plans secret. Adults are too cautious about everything. Catching bass is the most important part of our plan.

A few hours later we are catching lots of bass in the middle of Kuraya Pond, while along the high side of the pond, a line of teenagers carrying hoes on their shoulders walks past as they return to their homes in the plantation camp after a long day's work in the sugar fields. My sister, who accompanied us and is sitting on the shore, yells, "Eh, you guys, don't fall down in the water." The workers just walk on, looking happy that their workday is done. Plantation mules have the same hurried disposition when returning to the stables. No one is bothered with thoughts of two boys floating in a makeshift canoe in the middle of a large pond.

My friend and I are having a hell of a time, laughing and shouting, with fish flopping on the floor of the canoe. We even have to kick fish out of way in order to make space for our feet.

Eventually I notice the darkness creeping up on us. I lean over one side of the canoe to pull aboard the stone anchor. In doing so, the canoe takes on some water. My friend tries to counterbalance this lurch, but makes matters worse and water comes in from the other side. Suddenly, lots of water comes crashing into the canoe and we are swamped. It is so sudden that we each still have our paddles in our hands.

The canoe sinks, though the lightweight outrigger made of hau remains afloat. With our paddles in hand, we dog paddle around the outrigger and yell for help. The workers walking home alongside the pond continue trudging on and never look back.

We dog paddle to the shoreline, but without any of our fish or fishing gear, which sank. We look at each other, laugh out loud and begin heading for home. Looking back into the pond while walking along the cane field road, we notice the tiny canoe is submerged. Had we stayed in the pond swimming around the outrigger overnight, no one would have known to come to rescue us until two boys were missing during a headcount at home.

Happy to be alive, we skip home, knowing that we can make more bamboo fishing poles and another canoe. But next time I will be a better swimmer. I go back to Kuraya Pond the next day to learn the Australian crawl.

≈ ≈ ≈

Life goes on, in my absence the fish get bigger and I master the Australian crawl.

One day I swim to the area of the sunken canoe but cannot find it. The next day I make a bigger canoe from the leftover iron under our house and patch every hole and crevice. I go to the bamboo farm and get a longer pole and straighten it out by myself over a fire. My friend and I carry the canoe back to Kuraya Pond and go fishing in the deep water. We catch a lot of fish and we don't capsize our new canoe. Even if we did, we know we can easily get to shore because now we know how to swim.

Chapter 8
The Ghost of Felix

*M*other believed that drinking the blood of the koi fish was an antidote for any ailment, and she drank some periodically to keep herself strong. It must have helped her — to raise 13 children took a lot of energy.

One evening after work, my father prepared to go koi fishing for Mother. She fried a bit of maguro fish for him to use as bait, including a small piece of the blood-red central part of the body to enhance the bait smell. She mixed it with granulated pig mush and carefully wrapped the gourmet fish food in a ball in the remnants of an old torn shirt. We kept worn-out clothing as rags in a barrel for such uses.

Father looked around for someone to keep him company on his fishing trip.

"Iko ya. Da're ikitai, ka." ("Let's go! Who wants to go?") my father called out.

The only kid around was me.

None of my older brothers seemed to be around. They

might have been out playing with the neighborhood gang or maybe they had gone fishing on their own. Sometimes they just hid when they heard him calling. At 8 years old, I was excluded from my brothers' excursions because I was looked upon as a baby, someone to be looked after, too slow to run from any danger the group might encounter. My sisters were never taken on any trips outside of our village when they were young.

"Watashi iki-tai desho." ("I would love to go,") I said, excitedly.

I was eager to go on this adult kind of trip with my father. I came out from the kitchen with the fish bait and a small bento box that contained several things for my father to eat for dinner.

Father stored his huge throw net in a barley bag, ready for a trip like this. Although I was small and young, I felt strong enough to carry the heavy throw net, but Father put the bait, the bento and a bottle of water into the bag and carried it himself. I took hold of an empty barley bag to hold the fish we would catch, and off we went to get koi for my mother.

It normally took about 30 minutes to walk to Obake Pond (now called Kipu Falls). With me to look after it would take longer, but Father didn't mind. It felt much better to me to go out into the darkness with a companion. Maybe Father felt that way too.

At Obake Pond, we placed our supplies on a large rock on the edge of the water. Father put some pebbles in the cloth bait bag to weigh it down, then threw it about eight yards into the lake. The bag gurgled and absorbed water and slowly sank down. "The koi will smell this and linger around it, hoping to get a bite to eat," Father told me. We readied the fishing net, then settled down to wait for the fish to bite.

Father squatted down and took out a bag of Durham tobacco. He deftly fingered a piece of rolling paper and spread some tobacco onto it, licked the edges of the paper with his tongue and rolled it into a very tight, pencil-like cigarette. He does this so well, even in the light of the moon, I thought. Father slipped the cigarette into his pocket for later.

Obake Pond, now called Kipu Falls

As the light from the crescent moon shimmered on the small waves created by the waterfall in the lake, we each ate a musubi (small piece of meat wrapped with seaweed on a block of rice), and a piece of dry sausage, savoring our meal and hoping the koi had gathered around the bait bag.

Father lit his cigarette. The light from the smoke reflected on his face, making a weird ghost-like appearance, but I felt safe because I knew that it was him. We sat in silence because talking was forbidden. Fish can hear sounds in and outside of the water and we didn't want to scare them away.

Father finished his smoke, then took off his shirt and pants, folded them and placed them neatly beside me, so I knew he was preparing to throw the fishing net into the water. Standing only in his underwear, he grabbed in his left hand a few strands of the net that were connected to the top of the net frame and used them as a handle of sorts.

He rose up and prepared for a mighty heave. With a huge swing, he flung the net. As it flew, it spread into a circle 10 yards into the water. The whole net sank down and Father jumped in, still holding the several strings that were connected to the net frame. The water was deep and Father was now swimming above the net. He flailed away with his arms, creating a lot of commotion. His plan was that the fish, in their desperation to get away from the ruckus he was causing, would become tangled in the pockets of the net.

He swam back to shore and began pulling on the string, slowly retrieving the net that was now shivering with captured koi. Father patted the smaller fish and threw them back in the water, mumbling some encouraging words to them. He probably was telling them to grow up and be ready for him later. Two of the fish were very large. He put them into the extra barley bag and handed it to me. I was the proud bagboy.

We climbed up the embankment and headed for home on the cane field road. We walked in silence and I struggled to keep up to his pace, as the load I was carrying felt like it was becoming heavier. In the darkness and moonlight I followed his shadow. I felt totally secure because I was with him.

Felix

We were walking on Kipu Road, the main thoroughfare between the Obake Pond and the settlement of sugar plantation camps where we lived. Bordered by towering Norfolk pine trees on either side of the roadway, Kipu Road was normally cool and shady during the day. We children always avoided it at night lest we bump into the ghost of Felix, who frequented that road in the dark.

My painting of mile-long Kipu Road that was bordered by towering Norfolk pine trees. This is where the ghost of Felix was known to walk at night.

As we walked past Turning Pond, Father began talking to someone on his right. I heard the murmur of the conversation, but dared not turn my head to see who this stranger was. Through my peripheral vision I saw the faint form of a man-like figure walking stride-by-stride next to my father.

Father spoke to this shadowy figure in Pidgin Filipino, one of several dialects my father knew. The shadow did not utter a word, but I heard it grunt in agreement or disagreement. Father invited the shadow to our home to partake in his homemade sake. The shadow did not accept the invitation.

Shortly the conversation ceased and I felt that our company had left the scene. I glanced to the right and saw that we were almost at the end of Kipu Road.

When we got home, I corralled my father and asked him about the character who had walked with us. Father was reluctant to talk about it at first. Little by little he told me the man's name was Felix. They had been friends and Felix had died tragically. Felix had been crushed by a sugar plantation locomotive that he had been signaling, to help it back up. He was fatally squeezed between the engine and an empty train car.

Before he was killed, Felix had lived three doors down from our home in a house with three other bachelors. No one, including his Filipino friends, knew his last name. On the plantation he was known only as Number 75, which was his bango number, the number assigned to employees by the plantation and worn on a small piece of metal on a chain around the neck.

Felix had come to Kauai from the Philippines to work

in the sugarcane fields. He was not married and had left his family in the province of Ilocos Norte. He had worked as a "cut cane" man, the physically demanding job of cutting 15-foot-tall cane stalks with a machete for nine hours a day. His plan had been to make enough money to return to his homeland and live a life of luxury in his village.

Possibly the worst part of Felix's passing was that because his last name wasn't known, the plantation owner had no way to contact his kin in the Philippines. Mr. Rice had no alternative other than to bury Felix in the Kipu Cemetery, in the upper section where most of the other Filipino workers were buried.

≈ ≈ ≈

A handful of years ago, my brother William and I got permission from the Kipu Ranch management to visit Kipu Cemetery. We found it overgrown with thorny raspberry vines and the forest was encroaching. Most of the plots in the Japanese section of the cemetery had been exhumed and the bodies taken to a better cemetery by descendants. The Filipino burial plots are still there on the upper level, overgrown with weeds.

When he was alive, Father always cleaned up his best friend's tombstone in the Japanese section of the cemetery and directed the workers to attend to the Filipino section. But Father is gone now and Kipu Plantation closed many years ago.

I have visited often in the decades since I left Kauai to attend college, but I only go on Kipu Road in the daytime. I don't take a chance at night because with Father gone,

Felix might want to contact Father's immediate kin. I am now a senior citizen and running is not easy to do.

Hardly anyone walks on Kipu Road now, preferring to zoom by in vehicles. I know Felix's body is buried, but I wonder if his spirit continues to keep its lonely vigil on Kipu Road.

Chapter 9
Mokihana

As a boy, I enjoyed climbing to the top of the 2,300-foot-high Haupu Mountain that towered over our small plantation camp. It's an extremely steep and arduous ascent with only faint trails created by wild pigs to guide one's way. You have to make your own trail by grabbing branches and small shrubs to pull yourself up, while being careful that they don't detach into your hands. If you slip and fall, that's the end of you.

I climbed this grand mountain many times to explore the treasures this monolith held. My favorite reason for climbing Haupu was to find mokihana, a fragrant berry that grows in only three locations on the island.

When mokihana is in season, the distinct fragrance wafts through the air, exhorting climbers to complete their trek. Scaling Haupu was always worth the effort for the prize of mokihana berries, especially in mid-March, when the berries matured. Their fragrance resembles nothing I've encountered during my years on this planet, however, the smells of licorice and anise are close.

When you string mokihana berries with a needle to make a lei and include maile (a vine-like plant with aromatic leaves), your mokihana lei becomes the regal symbol of Kauai. None of the other Hawaiian islands can duplicate this treat because it is said that Kauai is the only island where mokihana grows.

When my daughter, Lois-Ann, was 5 years old, our family lived in Hilo on Hawaii Island, also known as the Big Island. I wondered if the mokihana trees of my youth still existed on the slopes of Haupu Mountain.

I returned to Kipu to follow up on this lingering memory. We climbed Haupu until we reached the forest of eucalyptus trees that I recalled from my youth. But I realized for safety reasons, I could not take my daughter to the top of the mountain, where mokihana dwelled along cliffs. We stopped for a light lunch and I pointed out the path that we took in my younger days to reach groves of guava and mountain apple trees. I told Lois-Ann that in those days we picked fresh fruits right off the trees and drank spring water for lunch.

One year, I asked a calabash cousin (a legally unrelated person who is treated as a family member), from Kekaha on the west side of Kauai to get me some mokihana berries during the season. To my surprise, she sent me quite a few. I diligently strung them into a lei and wore it with much delight, took photos of it, then sent the lei to my older brother, William, in Seattle. I wonder if the fragrance of mokihana berries ignited his boyhood memories as it did mine.

The thrill of finding mokihana remains with me to

this day, a lifetime past my childhood on Kauai. Boyhood
dreams never expire.

Haupu Mountain, rising 2,300 feet above Kipu.
Photo by Pamela Varma Brown

Chapter 10
Kipu's First Telephone

*W*hen I was a boy, the telephone company from Lihue came looking for a likely spot to install the very first telephone in Rice Camp, the sugar plantation housing complex in Kipu where I grew up.

The telephone company chose the Silva house, a large, centrally-located residence with a patio and big yard with ulu (breadfruit) trees, common mango trees, lots of coconut trees and a green carpet of centipede grass with a fence of hibiscus around it.

Even though Mr. Silva was the plantation overseer, he had nothing to say about the telephone matter. The plantation owner, whose rule was absolute, gave his approval, and a wooden box was nailed to the wall of the Silva home. There was now a phone in Rice Camp and it was for everybody's use.

But there was a problem: How would we let someone know that a call was for them? One suggestion was that the young Silva son could personally visit a family when a call came in for them. The boy was an adolescent in high school and this idea didn't sit well with him.

Instead someone decided that the phone ring would follow international Morse code, which is a series of dots and dashes or "dits" and "dahs," to be tooted by a horn. Each plantation employee had a bango number but it was decided that it would be too complex to use because it would involve too many "dit dits." So the first letter of each family's last name would be used. For example, Yamanaka would be represented by Morse code for the letter Y or "dah dit dah dah."

Let me run through a phone call. The Lihue office of the telephone company receives a call meant for the Yamanaka household about a pending funeral to be held at the Hosoi Mortuary. The Lihue office contacts the Silva telephone and Mrs. Silva receives the call. She sets the phone down on the holding pedestal and toots the loud horn with a "dah dit dah dah." I hear the horn from our garden and know the phone call is for our family. I rush home and let my mother know that I will run over to the Silva house to receive the call. I go to the phone booth on the side of the Silva house, take the call and the message is completed.

All callers knew that it took time to complete a call, so everyone knew that only urgent calls should be made by telephone. In non-emergency situations, walking to the house and passing the message in person was a better way of communicating.

In fact, there was hardly any use of a phone in those days. No one used it as a means of gabbing. If you wanted to pass on information, you would walk to that person's house and let him know what you had to say.

In our plantation camp, there was a bit of confusion with all the horn tooting because the plantation let out its own toot at 6 a.m. by releasing steam from a compressor to signal workers that it was time to start the day's work.

Nevertheless, now Rice Camp was in touch with the world: a telephone for everyone's use. What a blessing it was for the camp families.

Chapter 11
Hole Hole Bushi

While I was busy making canoes and going to school, my mother worked on and off in the sugar cane fields, like a lot of the other mothers did. Of course as a child, I wasn't fully aware of this hardship.

The women's work was to strip the dry leaves from the cane stalks, so that men on the "cut cane" crews could more easily cut the stalks into foot-long pieces. Japanese women in the fields would often sing a folk song named "Hole Hole Bushi" (pronounced "holay, holay booshee"), while performing this labor-intensive task. "Hole hole" is the Hawaiian term for the dried sugar cane leaves, and "bushi" is the Japanese word for melody or tune.

It is said that different lyrics were sung on each of the islands, but the theme was the same, bemoaning long days in the hot sun, doing hard manual labor.

Of course, in all their years living near and working for the sugar plantation, I am sure my parents heard this song and its varying verses, but they never told me anything about it directly. Over the years, however, I heard from many people older than me that the "Hole Hole Bushi" song existed and that women sang it often, expressing their longing for a better life.

Here is one of the translations I have heard over the years:

> *My husband cuts the cane stalks,*
> *And I trim the leaves,*
> *With sweat and tears we both work,*
> *For our means*

Women also worked kalai (hoeing) between the rows of cane to till the soil and to make it easier for children to pull the weeds that otherwise could crowd out the growing cane. My mother did this type of work, too. The pay was 25 cents per day for kalai.

Although I was too young to remember, my mother probably took me into the fields while working, as most mothers did, unless there was an older sibling who could stay home and watch the younger children.

All the babies who were brought into the fields were left in a certain place, often on a lauhala (leaf) mat under a tarp of some sort, to shield their skin from the strong Hawaiian sun. The biggest danger was centipedes that crawl under the mats during the day to seek darkness. The fields were littered with those biting pests. A bite from a centipede on an infant would be a hospital case because that creature's venom is quite toxic.

Every now and then, someone would go to feed the babies. The young water boy who worked for the plantation also made periodic visits to the place where the babies were.

The water boy collected fresh spring water from the irrigation ditches. (We used to drink that irrigation ditch water — that was normal for us.) The water boy would walk slowly from one row of sugar cane to another, barely visible along the tall stalks with their bright green leaves, as he carried his 60-pound bucket of water. As he walked up beside the employees, he would dip his cup into the bucket and give you water if you wanted some.

Burn Days

Immediately before harvest time were the "burn days," the days the cane fields were set on fire to burn off all but the sugar cane stalk itself, because the plantations had no use for the rest of the plant. Oh, what a sight that was for a young boy! It was a huge blaze, a lot of smoke. We were lucky that our home was upwind from the smoke. Other families had a lot of ash fall into their yards and had to clean it up after burn days.

Before I came of age, laws had changed so that no one younger than 15 could be hired. When I made 15, I went to work.

Instead of sugar, I worked for a pineapple plantation, weeding the fields and picking pineapple. We worked in a long row and we boys used to pick with both hands. There was a technique to it. You picked a pineapple with each hand, held each fruit at the crown and snapped your wrist. The pineapples would snap off and fall onto a conveyor belt going into a waiting truck. You had to wear long gloves that stretched up your arm, to protect yourself from the sharp, pointy leaves of the crown.

While I was working in the pineapple fields, it never occurred to me that I would go to college. But I did. I know that when that day came, my mother was very proud.

Chapter 12
My First and Last Cockfight

In the neighborhood where I grew up, Filipino families were mixed in with us Japanese. Originally, when immigrants from all over the world came to Kauai to work for the sugar plantations, starting in the mid-1800s, each ethnic group was provided housing separate from the other cultures. I don't know if this was more for the convenience of the employees or for the plantations, but that's how it was.

Over time, many people returned to their home country or quit sugar as their employment and found living quarters elsewhere. New laborers were interspersed wherever there was an available house.

That's how our next-door neighbors came to be bachelors Antone and Lazario from Ilocos Norte in the Philippines. When Antone saw the "Hawayanos" who returned to the Philippines from Hawaii with their show of wealth and the women they attracted, he decided to come to Hawaii himself. He was assigned to work at the Kipu Sugar Plantation.

Antone and Lazario worked long hours, leaving the house in the darkness of morning and returning around 6 p.m. Antone was a "cut cane" man, cutting 15-foot-tall stalks of sugar cane with a machete or cane knife all day. It was very hard work.

At home, he tested the sharpness of his two knives by slicing at the cane plants in his backyard. When I was a child, I worried that if Antone ever got angry at me, he would send my head rolling with one slash. Lucky for me that both Lazario and Antone were very kind men.

I'll always remember Antone relaxing while smoking his Toscano cigars. He had one in his mouth whenever he was not working. Despite how hard they worked for the plantation, when they were relaxing, I would sometimes hear Antone or Lazario say to one another, *"Kasla glorya ti Hawaii!"* "Hawaii is like a paradise!"

The Cockfight

The two men tethered roosters outside in their dirt yard. Each rooster had a little corrugated iron house and a can of water. These birds crowed and crowed throughout the day. I imagine this constant crowing was a call for dominance over hens, but Antone and Lazario raised no hens, so I suppose all the crowing was in vain.

When the two men came home from work each night, I heard the clanking sound of them refilling the roosters' cans of water. They also tossed a handful of scratch feed on the ground. The men seemed to feed their chickens more carefully than they fed themselves. It looked to me like the men ate primarily rice, sharing some nightly with the cat that lived on their porch.

On Sunday nights, Antone and Lazario joined other Filipinos for cockfights in which roosters were made to battle each other while wearing metal spurs on their legs to harm one another. Spectators placed bets on the birds they thought would win. Cockfighting was made illegal in 1884 in Hawaii but for many years it was done on a regular basis in semi-secret.

One Sunday afternoon when I was about 10 years old, I attended a baseball game at the Kipu baseball park, which bordered the arena where cockfights were held. Children were only allowed into the cockfights accompanied by an adult, so I had never seen one before. I was drawn toward the arena by the smell of food, when I saw Antone sitting on the top of a gate.

He led me over to the concessions where people under two tents were serving Filipino food. He ordered a mixed plate with adobo (chicken or pork stewed in vinegar, garlic and soy sauce), pinakbet (mixed vegetables steamed in fish or shrimp sauce) and a generous scoop of rice. We weren't given a fork, spoon or chopsticks so Antone told me to eat with my fingers like the men around us did. I noticed Antone paying a lot of attention to a pretty Filipina woman who was serving meals behind the counter. Then he led me into the arena so I could wander about while he returned to sitting on the gate railing, where he was stationed as the lookout.

Three-tiered bleachers circled the arena. Handlers brought their roosters into the arena and gently threw them into the air. Most of the birds were red. The few white ones stood out, and the black ones seemed most menacing. With wings flapping, knives in sheaths attached to their legs, each rooster let out a mighty crow while attempting to kill one another.

A ringmaster walked around inside the arena collecting bets. He had no notebook for the recording of names and bet amounts, and seemed unconcerned about that kind of problem. I guessed that he had a keen memory and could remember all of the details. Everyone seemed unworried about the illegality of chicken fights, and the jabbering seemed to intensify as the bets were hollered to the ringmaster.

Suddenly the noise stopped. From atop his fencepost perch, Antone blew his referee-type whistle repeatedly to signal that a police raid was coming. He closed the gate, men picked up their bets and within seconds the whole arena looked like a carnival with men walking nonchalantly around the concessions. It was so smooth and organized.

The policeman, Sgt. Manaya, drove his Ford Model A slowly on the single-lane road near the baseball park and eucalyptus grove, then circled around the ballpark and reentered the one-way road to the arena. He was a big Hawaiian, at 6-foot-3 and 250 pounds. No one wanted to fight this man. In those years, a policeman was given total respect from everyone.

Sgt. Manaya acted like he had no intention of stopping and that he was only driving by to find something to eat. He picked up a bottle of strawberry soda and some hot dogs, then got back into his car, driving past the gate to the arena with a knowing smile on his face.

Once he was out of sight, the ringmaster checked to

make sure none of the roosters had been tampered with, men conversed with each other in Ilocano, and the fights continued.

It was a violent activity and one rooster was almost always killed in each round. Handlers picked up the birds and the dead rooster became the property of the winner. The ringmaster walked around and gathered the cash. He knew exactly what amount to give or collect. No one disputed his approach, so I guess all of the bets were correct.

Every Sunday night Antone returned home, sometimes with the roosters he brought to the fights and sometimes with a dead chicken that was made into adobo. I was told that a fighting rooster is very tough and sinewy but a few slices of green papaya tenderizes the meat and makes it quite appetizing.

Such was life for Antone, Lazario and most of the unskilled Filipino laborers, or "sakadas," who worked for the sugar plantations. Of the approximately 112,000 Filipinos who came to Hawaii for work, about 40 percent returned to their homeland. I can almost hear them enthusiastically telling the new recruits, *"Kasla glorya ti Hawaii!"* Hawaii was paradise for them.

Chapter 13
The Skull

*I*t all started as a fun trip for the Boy Scouts of Troop 12 to Kipu Kai, the pristine beach about two miles southwest of our plantation camp. To get there, we hiked on a trail that took us through a gap in the mountains, across privately-owned land, then down to the beach. We had been given permission to stay overnight in several cottages that dotted the shoreline.

After unloading the gear at one of the cottages, we grabbed our spear fishing equipment and headed for the lagoon. Amidst shouts of bravado, our group of energetic Scouts speared manini (surgeonfish), mamo (sergeant fish) and all kinds of other fish.

A few of the boys started a fire between some rocks, preparing for a feast of pulehu (broiled) fish. Someone had brought some rice, and we had a wonderful meal.

Before long, evening came, the moon rose and moonbeams lit up the mountains. Someone suggested that we walk over to the next valley to look for goats. Energized by our meal of barbecued fish, we all agreed.

We trotted along the sand dunes, between the kiawe trees and over small hillsides looking for goats, but we didn't find any. Before long, we found ourselves in the next valley, Mahaulepu, the beginning of Kauai's south shore.

As the moonlight illuminated the beach, we noticed what appeared to be a number of white balls floating in the sand, on a plateau above the beach. When we got closer, we realized that those white balls were human skulls.

Curious, we crept closer and saw more than skulls. There were entire skeletons buried in the sand. It looked like there had been some sort of slaughter on the beach.

I had heard tales of Hawaiian warriors who had tried to wrest control of the island about 150 years ago from Kauai's last independent king. Most of the invaders drowned in the ocean channel between Oahu and Kauai, when they were confronted by a huge storm. But a few of the warriors made landfall on Kauai's south shore, where, exhausted, they fell asleep on the beach. Just before dawn, some Kauai people discovered the invaders and slaughtered almost all of them.

I wondered if these were the bones of those warriors. I picked up one of the skulls, thinking I would take it home as a souvenir. No one else dared to handle those skeletons for fear of being spooked at night, but I didn't know any better. I hid the skull in my knapsack. No one saw me do this. I thought maybe I would scare someone at home with my find.

Finally, we boys had enough of bones and decided to go back to the cottage. I was last in the group. I was always last in our marching activities, anyway, so no one paid any attention to my position in the pack. I was glad because I knew our Scoutmaster would not approve of my new cargo.

The next day we went spear fishing and swimming again in the lagoon in front of the cottage. We had a great time, even spearing some lobsters in shallow holes in the ocean. Around noon, we stuffed some lobster and fish in our backpacks and headed uphill to return to our plantation camp.

When I walked in the house, I took my fish and lobsters out of my backpack, and then placed the skull on the kitchen table. Mother was none too pleased when she saw the skull. She was very superstitious and immediately asked me where I found it. I described the beach filled with warriors' bones. She was very agitated, and told me I had desecrated burial grounds by taking one of the skulls. I was loathe to let go of my treasure yet, so I simply stomped off to my bedroom, leaving the skull on the table.

That night as I lay in bed, I felt the whole house begin shaking. I got out of bed and worked my way to the kitchen. There on the kitchen table where I had left the skull on display, that shiny dome was also shaking. Mother must have felt the shaking as well, because she woke up, came to the kitchen and scolded me. She demanded that I take the skull back to Mahaulepu.

I mulled over how I could possibly return the skull, now that I saw what terror it was bringing to our home. That area of Mahaulepu was privately-owned at the time, and only groups like the Boy Scouts would be given permission to go there. How could I possibly tell the Scoutmaster why I wanted to go back? There had to be a way.

Early the next morning, I put on my Boy Scout uniform, thinking that would make it easier to get a ride to the end of the approximately five miles of dirt road to the hillside that locked in the valley.

I got a ride from Seki Camp to the main road. My next ride was to the junction of Koloa. From there I hitchhiked to the sea coast. A visitor picked me up and drove me to the hillside of Mahaulepu Valley. I hiked along the sand dunes until I reached the area of beach where all the skeletons were.

Carefully, I took the skull out of my backpack and returned it to be with the other bones.

"Rest in peace," I said, and apologized for my actions.

With this heavy burden lifted, I returned home before sunset and slept well into the night. From that point on, I never touched another bone in any Hawaiian cemetery of any kind. When it came to bones, I was now as superstitious as my mother.

Chapter 14
Return of the Spirits

*O*ne August morning, when I was 6 years old, our entire village climbed the slopes of Haupu Mountain to clean the community cemetery, as we did every Obon season. We carried water in gallon jugs to scrub green moss off the gravestones and pulled weeds. There were quite a few O-Jizo markers scattered around the cemetery indicating that a lot of children died at a young age. O-Jizo is an enlightened being whose likeness is believed to protect children as their spirits journey to heaven.

Father was the gravestone carver for our village, and he also chiseled the names, birth and death dates on the stones. Our family had no gravestones yet, so we were cleaning two stones belonging to another family that were protected by a small wooden structure that was painted plantation green. The stones had Japanese calligraphy carved on them that I could not read.

"Whose grave is this?" I asked, turning to Father.

"Hara-san," he said. ("San" is a Japanese title of respect.)

I was not aware of Hara-san from the village, but Father explained that this couple came as Issei (first generation immigrants from Japan) from Yamaguchi-ken (the state of Yamaguchi). Mr. Hara worked for two contractual periods at the Kipu Sugar Plantation and died in a tragic industrial accident. Hara-san was Father's co-worker and since no one came to claim the body, my father assumed the responsibility.

Mrs. Hara was allowed by the plantation manager to remain in the plantation home she had occupied with her family. Her neighbors provided moral support for her and her two children. She tended her garden every day, rain or shine.

Once, when Mrs. Hara had not been seen in her garden for several days, my father went to investigate. He found Mrs. Hara sick in bed with a high fever and showing signs of serious complications. One week later, the plantation doctor diagnosed her with pneumonia. She died a few days later.

When Mrs. Hara died, it was much too expensive to send her remains to Japan for internment, so Father buried her alongside her husband, made the gravestone, and built a small house over the gravestones. The hut was the only one in the whole cemetery. The couple's two children were sent to live with relatives in Honolulu.

I learned this is why our family maintained the Hara burial site every year during Obon season.

Obon Festival

In Japanese tradition, the Bon or Obon Festival is a time when spirits of the departed come to visit loved ones. Most of the immigrants in the two plantation camps where I grew up in Kipu were originally from Hiroshima or Yamaguchi-ken. They lived their lives as closely as possible to what they knew from the old country, making Obon season an event shared by the community as a whole.

During Obon, the first day was devoted to each family as they welcomed the spirits of departed loved ones to their homes, with the distinct smell of senko (thin sticks of Japanese incense) wafting in the air. My parents called to spirits from Mother's hometown of Heigun, Japan. The welcome was also extended to the Hara family spirits.

Mother, who was pregnant with her twelfth child, clanged bells with an overwhelming intensity. Father chanted his Buddhist mantra in front of the Butsudan, the household-size Buddhist shrine we had in our home. I am sure that the spirits heard this clamor from afar.

The spirits were fed well with offerings of rice and tea by my mother that were double the size of her daily gifts to the spirits. She also offered a dish of takuwan (pickled daikon radish) made from the turnips she grew in her garden. Mother also presented broiled shoyu koi fish that Father caught in Obake Pond. We Yamanaka children could only stand in the doorway and wonder if this exotic behavior included us.

One time, I happened to be in the doorway and saw my mother eating the cup of rice that she had placed on the Butsudan the previous day. Much later I learned that spirits are not like living human beings, and that although they partake in offerings, they leave the physical evidence. Eating the leftover rice is considered particularly beneficial for humans to have a good life.

The Shin Buddhist minister made a visit to each family and said a prayer for each. The sight of the minister was awe-inspiring. He was a very big Japanese person, wearing his black kimono, carrying his ministry symbols, very long black beads around his neck, his Jizo grasped in his hand, and clomping to each house noisily in his getta (traditional Japanese wooden-soled shoes).

Each household anticipated the minister's arrival with properly laid out zabuton (traditional Japanese floor cushions) on the second tier of the lanai (balcony). Although he had visited several other homes before arriving at ours, the minister's white tabi (split-toe Japanese socks) on both feet were immaculately clean. It can be concluded that each household did some serious scrubbing in preparation for his arrival.

When the minister came to the porch, he was treated with such reverence that he was greeted with the deepest bow that I ever saw. As he chanted deeply between the very loud sounds of his inhalations, he wrung his Buddhist beads, bowed and looked into the eyes of the Buddha in the Butsudan. He repeated this scene in every home, mollifying the spirits in each household.

Bon Dance & Toro Nagashi

The following Saturday was declared a holiday. At 6 a.m., everyone gathered at the community hall in preparation for the minister to lead the half-mile march to the mountain cemetery to take the spirits there to visit the dead. Paper lanterns fluttered in the breeze and the colorful scene was filled with anticipation. The heads of each family marched behind him, followed by the mothers, then the children. When the minister reached the halfway point, marked by a grove of guava trees, the last of the children started off from the horse stables, which was the staging place. The spirits had no trouble finding the path, since an advance party had already gone ahead and lit lots of incense.

The minister offered a prayer at the gates of the cemetery, then looked up, as if to include all of the Huleia region as his audience. His beseeching sounds reverberated to the mountain top, rolling up to the sentinels of the Haupu Range. The spirits were already there, easily finding their gravestones, and happy to see that everything was spruced up to their satisfaction. After more senko lighting, more prayers and more offerings for the dead, everyone marched back to the community hall for that evening's celebratory Bon dance.

Outside the community hall, a yagura (a high wooden stand) had been constructed in the middle of the lot, around which the ceremonial Bon dance was held. During a Bon dance, everyone danced to traditional Japanese songs, slowly circling the yagura. One of the common dance melodies was the Japanese folk song, "Tanko Bushi."

The sounds of drums and "Tanko Bushi" boomed out into the still night air. The light of the moon silhouetted the Haupu Mountain Range. The mountain cemetery was a beautiful sight of lighted lanterns swaying in the gentle tradewinds.

On Sunday, with the spirits still thought to be lingering in the area, the Obon celebration concluded with an event that helps the spirits return to the heavens, a ceremony named toro nagashi. Small paper boats, rigged with sails, each carrying a lighted candle, were slowly released into Kuraya Pond. The tradewinds blew in whispering puffs as the armada of sailboats rippled their way to the middle of the pond, then washed ashore on the small island in the middle of the pond or settled on the neki reeds.

≈ ≈ ≈

As an adult in 1990, I found myself in Hiroshima, Japan, during the peak of Obon season. The train stations were jammed with people moving in and out of Hiroshima. Obon is a national holiday in Japan, and millions travel to celebrate this event.

Upon my return to Hawaii, I visited Kauai and made a trip to Kipu. The sugar fields were gone, replaced by a cattle ranch. My brother and I walked up to the former cemetery. The entry was still discernible, marked by some stone carvings. We had to climb over wild and invasive red berry vines to enter.

The change was astounding. The cemetery was an overgrown patch of eucalyptus trees, lantana and other noxious weeds. The Hara hut was gone but the gravestones were still there, leaning backward, displaced and abandoned. The gravestones my father carved were sinking into the earth as the forest reclaimed the land, as were the O-Jizo statues, which were made of wood.

Nearly 80 years ago I was there, helping my father and our community clean gravestones in preparation for the season of Obon. Now Kipu Cemetery has been absorbed by the Haupu Mountain Range. Those of us who lived in Kipu will always remember our Obon celebrations, complete with Bon dances and toro nagashi ceremonies. We'll also remember the Kipu Sugar Plantation cemetery on the slopes of Haupu Mountain.

Chapter 15
The Death of Mr. Matsuo

*M*en live and die on Earth, but at Kipu Sugar Plantation, fatalities were rare. Men were frequently injured with things like a strained back, a cut from a scythe or from sharp sugar cane leaves. But the case of Mr. Matsuo was most grave. It left a mark deep on my soul, as I was a young boy when it happened.

Mr. Matsuo had arrived in Hawaii as a young man who wanted to make a fortune and return to Japan. As he got older, he alleviated his loneliness by acquiring a picture bride and fathering children from that union. The children were raised as Americans, so it would have been difficult for them to return to Japan.

Mr. Matsuo had been working toward his new American dream on the day he lost his life. He was bludgeoned by a runaway cane car when the brakes failed. There was no opportunity for him to jump away and dodge this rolling car as the terrain was downhill. He was 52 years old and was survived by his wife, Michiko, three daughters and two sons.

As the eldest son, the burden of the family fell on Stanley Matsuo, and he rightfully assumed that role. Stanley had been attending the University of Washington and was majoring in engineering. Elders in Mr. Matsuo's Japanese hometown of Yamaguchi urged that Mr. Matsuo's body be cremated and his ashes sent for burial in the family plots at Yosaku Temple. However, Stanely argued for burial in Kipu, where his father had been pursuing his American dream. Michiko eventually agreed, and Kipu was chosen for the final rites. All of Mr. Matsuo's children had left Kipu after high school to attend college on the Mainland but they all came back to attend their father's funeral.

Because of Father's involvement as gravestone cutter for our village, and because our plantation camp community was so small, I learned of Mr. Matsuo's demise and attended his funeral service. It was my first time to attend such a solemn event. It was held in the traditional Japanese style. All these many years later, the images remain seared in my mind.

≈ ≈ ≈

In a Japanese funeral, chants tell of beliefs that one is born into a good world where life should be for good deeds. Reverend Shindo's chants told of Mr. Matsuo's service to the Kipu Sugar Plantation.

The entire community hall was deathly silent with the exception of the reverend's voice and the clang of the gong that accompanied his chanting. Reverend Shindo's wailing reverberated up to the Haupu Mountain Range, calling for Kami (God in the Shinto religion) to come forth and lead our group of mourners into the heavenly world where all of Mr. Matsuo's ancestors dwelled.

Earlier, the minister had placed his portable kamidana (miniature household altar) in the front portion of the hall. Now he placed large and small mochi (Japanese rice cake) with a mikan (tangerine) on top. He tapped the gong three times and began chanting again. I watched as he flicked a bamboo branch to and fro, as if to clear a path to the world of Kami. He repeated this ritual three times to be sure that this avenue was open to Mr. Matsuo. Kami apparently heard his calls and sent his spirits down to Kipu to escort Mr. Matsuo to the heavenly beyond.

Now the only thing remaining of Mr. Matsuo here on earth was his body. The plantation owner provided a horse-drawn carriage to take the body to the mountainside Kipu Cemetery. The Japanese custom generally was to cremate the body, but there was no crematorium in Kipu. Instead, a rectangular six-foot hole was dug by the funeral committee; the solemn attendees walked behind the carriage with the minister leading the group.

Curious how Mr. Matsuo's body was to be handled, I watched closely as Reverend Shindo stopped at the gates of the stately torii (traditional Japanese gate at sacred places) at the entrance of the cemetery. He carried a bell, chimed it three times and asked permission from the spirits to enter. Then our group proceeded.

The pallbearers grasped the coffin and headed for the gravesite, while the reverend's chanting continued. Everyone shuffled into position, with me at the front, watching to make sure I learned how this was done, as the coffin was lowered to the bottom. The stillness of the air indicated that Mr. Matsuo's spirit was accepted into Nirvana. Suddenly, an unusual gust of wind blew past the tops of the eucalyptus trees. Kami was making his presence known.

≈ ≈ ≈

After the funeral, Stanley dropped out of school to assume care of his mother and other responsibilities at home. He could not find a suitable job for himself in Kipu, so he moved to Lihue (a 15-minute drive by car today, but it seemed a much farther distance in those days), to start his own import business. He catered to the growing need for Japanese goods for the increasing number of workers coming to Kauai from Japan.

≈ ≈ ≈

Sometime in the 1980s, a reunion for former Kipu residents was held, with hundreds of people attending. We gathered in front of the place where the community hall once stood. After taking a group photograph, our group walked the mile on pine tree-lined Kipu Road to Rice Camp, then to Kipu Kai, then through the tunnel that Grove Farm Company built through the mountain to allow cane haul trucks to travel faster between Puhi and Koloa.

Mr. Matsuo never got to walk through that tunnel, a one-of-a-kind on Kauai that still exists today. Places like the tunnel were off-limits for the local people unless their plantation work required their presence there.

But Mr. Matsuo can return to Kauai and Kipu each year during Obon season, when he will be welcomed back with open arms.

Chapter 16
A Piece of Home

In 1945, when I was 13 years old, Father fell off a truck while loading eucalyptus trees for the plantation. After the accident, he was permanently incapacitated due to a painful hip injury and could no longer work. Fortunately, my oldest siblings were already working in Honolulu and they helped defray some of the family's living expenses.

Seven years later, Father died from heart problems. He was 62 years old. Mother and the children still living at home were dutifully supported by our older brothers and sisters.

My father left this world without relaying much information about his life here on Earth. Bit by bit, I pieced together some of his adventures for this book from others who knew him, and from my own memories, yet for years I wanted to know more. I was only 20 years old when he died, and had not yet the insight to ask him directly about his life. I suppose not many young men do at that age.

≋ ≋ ≋

When I served on the U.S.S. Castor as a teleman (a petty officer performing clerical, coding and communications duties) during the Korean War after college, I had the opportunity to visit Wakayama, Japan, my father's birthplace. I was able to take shore leave to investigate what I could about my father's life before he came to Kauai.

I traveled by diesel train from Yokohama to Osaka, then another locomotive took me to the Wakayama Peninsula. English was not commonly used in Japan at that time, so I had to get information by pantomime. Fortunately, an office girl at the naval base had written my destination on a piece of paper for me in Katakana (Japanese phonetic writing).

When I got off the train, I showed a taxi driver a letter I had from my cousin Kusunojo, who was the first son of my father's oldest brother. The driver looked hesitantly at the return address on the letter and somehow I understood by his expression that the house was far out in the country.

Father's oldest brother had inherited this home, as was customary in Japan in those years. Kusunojo had inherited the house from his father. The modest farmhouse was a typical Japanese country home. Cooking was done on the dirt floor outside of the living area. These areas were under roof and a covered storage room was full of onions hanging from a rafter to dry out. The outhouse and a furoba (Japanese bathing structure) was located nearby.

Kusunojo did not know much about my father's family, but he walked me over to the local cemetery and showed me the gravestones of the Yamanaka kin. There were many granite-like headstones. He lit some incense sticks for each and clasped his Buddhist beads in prayer. In Japan, most of the deceased are buried in a family plot in their hometown. I bowed in prayer, hoping that I would be accepted by the spirits of my ancestors as a suitable stand-in for my father on this planet.

I concluded that my father had never had a desire to return to Wakayama. He had his large family on Kauai to attend to, and had no cash in reserve, anyway.

≈ ≈ ≈

Father has been gone for more than half a century now, but his legacy still remains. When I go to Kipu Falls, I can still see him in my mind's eye netting the large wild koi below the waterfall. I see him selling his burdock vegetable to the peddler, Mr. Kajiwara; I see him in his denim clothes limping to and fro after the accident. I see him expertly rolling his own tobacco, wetting the paper with a swipe of his tongue. Some of his calligraphy carvings on the gravestones in the hills of Haupu are still evident. In Kipu, the pohaku (stone) monument of plantation owner William Hyde Rice that Father carved, remains a tangible memory of his skills.

Father is buried in a cemetery in Kaneohe, Oahu. His last wish was to have the omamori pouch — that his mother had pressed into his hands on the docks of Yokohama the day he left Japan for Hawaii — be opened and its contents buried with him. The pouch contained soil from his home in Wakayama. Through 45 years of toil, falling in love, raising a large family and living on Kauai, Father kept that pouch safely with him. Though he never made it back to Japan, he was buried with a piece of home.

≈ ≈ ≈

I secretly vowed that I would do one more thing for Father. After I retired from the Department of Education, I made frequent trips to Japan, where I taught English. One summer I took a month's leave from my job and headed for the top of Mount Fuji, the highest mountain in Japan at 12,388 feet. One of the greatest aspirations of all Japanese people is to climb to the top of Mount Fuji. Thousands of Japanese make this pilgrimage each summer. From the seventh station to the tenth at the summit, the climb is steep. A rope is strung along the trails to assist climbers with the incline, but nothing was going to deter me from my goal.

Once at the top of the mountain, I scooped two small plastic containers of soil and brought them back to Hawaii. To enhance my vow to Father, I also made trips to Nara, the town where my cousin Kusunojo now lives in the farmhouse near Wakayama prefecture, and Heigun, my mother's birthplace. I scooped soil from both of those places, as well.

In a special memorial service in Honolulu, my older brother William scattered the soil from Nara and Mount Fuji on Father's grave.

My father, Kichijiro Yamanaka, came to Hawaii as a young man, died in Hawaii, is buried in Hawaii, and is surrounded by soil from his homeland. Father, you are a son of Hawaii and you created the opportunity for me to grow up on the Garden Island of Kauai . . . where my heart remains.

The pohaku (stone) monument my father carved in honor of Kipu Sugar Plantation's first owner, William Hyde Rice, is one of the last tangible memories of my father's time here on this earth.

Chapter 17
Mother's Farewell

*A*fter my father died and the last of my siblings moved out on their own, Mother loved her independence. When the time came for her to leave Kipu and move to the island of Oahu, where three of her children, and eventually her grandchildren, could look in on her, my eldest brother Sam provided a house for her.

One of her bedrooms was her Butsudan room, where, during prayer time, she rang the small bell, as she always had while living in Kipu, offered a bowl of hot rice to the spirits and ate the prior day's rice offering. A small portrait of my father graced the Butsudan, and I imagine she also offered a prayer for his soul.

Mother's small yard was planted with papaya, beans and squash growing in abundance, a reminder of all she had learned about self-reliance while living in Kipu. She didn't drive, and instead walked to the stores in her neighborhood. She loved her home and would often sit on a stool in her garage, cooling off in the tradewinds. It seems she had spent so many years doing things for her large family and being on call for all of us children, that she enjoyed this more relaxed pace in her later life.

Though most of her children lived in far places, from Milwaukee to Guam, all contributed to make her life comfortable.

≈ ≈ ≈

In 1983 at the age of 82, Mother was confined to a hospital bed for 21 days, the result of a heart condition stemming from diabetes. The doctors advised us that giving birth to many children had contributed to organ problems, and she had been unaware of drugs to minimize the symptoms of diabetes.

One day while in the hospital, Mother made it clear that she wanted her house to be put in order. She sent my sister, Doris, and me to clean it, and gave us specific orders to move the floor rugs from the living room into the closet. Once Doris and I arrived at the house, we forgot all about the floor rugs.

After straightening up the house, I was lying down drowsily on the living room couch while Doris napped in Mother's bedroom. I was awakened by the characteristic smell of Mother, as if she had brushed past me. Doris said she also felt the brushing. In retrospect, I believe Mother's spirit returned to the house to check up on us. It must be true, because when we returned to the hospital, she admonished us that we had not done what she told us to do. How else could she have known that we had forgotten about the rugs?

As Mother lay in that hospital bed, connected to life-giving tubes, she would constantly say, *"Ie ni itai"* ("I want to be home.") As each of us children came to see her for the last time, she recognized us, then looked straight up at the ceiling, repeating only, *"Ie ni itai."* We understood, but felt powerless to do anything.

Mother's final request was that after she died, she wanted to be taken by hearse for a farewell view of her home. Sam arranged this for her. Those present waited for her in the driveway as the hearse arrived. The back doors of the car were opened and Mother had her final look at her last home on this earth.

Mother's body was laid to rest peacefully under the shade of a large tree in the cool, breezy grounds of the cemetery. After the funeral service, all those who attended were fed in grand style, per Mother's request. There were heaps of food to the satisfaction of everyone. Her resting place is graced with flowers at all times, by her children, grandchildren and great-grandchildren.

Years later I scattered on Mother's grave some of the same soil that I brought home from Nara and Mount Fuji.

≈ ≈ ≈

My mother was a very simple woman. She came to Hawaii at age 15, never enrolled in the public schools of Hawaii and could not read or write in Japanese, nor in English. She could only write her name in Katakana, a basic form of Japanese characters.

But Mother had persistence. Somehow she learned how to cook and keep a houseful of 13 children. She became a genius at providing for a large family on a meager budget. Twice she was able to return to visit her birthplace in Japan. Each time she returned with appreciation of her life in Hawaii.

Mother's legacy lives on with all of her children. Bless our giant of a mother.

Chapter 18
Kipu Memories

*T*ime moves on in its own way, and I now find myself an 83-year-old man. Since leaving Kauai as an 18-year-old to attend college in Wisconsin, I have lived an active and fulfilling life. Yet my heart always returns to Kipu.

The sugar plantation that employed my father converted to raising cattle when the demand for beef became acute and growing sugar cane became more challenging. As sugar fields became pastures, the employee count of the plantation went from 300 to about four people, and the Yamanaka horde was no longer needed to help work the land. And so it was for other families, as well. Kipu became a ghost of the past.

This was truly a blessing in disguise. Just imagine working in the sugar fields for the rest of one's life after graduating from eighth grade.

We were fortunate in the Yamanaka family that we learned from our parents that persistence, and possibly stubbornness, are of tremendous value. After all, what can't be accomplished with those characteristics?

My older brothers and sisters attended school only until the eighth grade, after which they set out on their own paths and found their success, supporting our household as necessary as our parents got older. My younger siblings and I attended college. Our parents encouraged us, but of course we had no financial support from home, as there was no extra money.

All five Yamanaka boys gave military service to our country: four in the U.S. Army, and I served in the U.S. Navy. Fortunately, all five of us returned home safely without a scratch from the horrors of warfare, and continued on with our lives, some with the benefits of the GI Bill funding college educations.

≈ ≈ ≈

My life since leaving Kipu has been fruitful. After at-

tending the Milwaukee School of Technology, I transferred to the University of Wisconsin, Milwaukee and graduated with a teaching degree. I then was drafted into the Navy and served with 7th ServPac Fleet of the Pacific. My shore time was spent in places like Hong Kong, Singapore, Guam, Sasebo and Yokosuka, whetting my appetite for world traveling.

I married Jean and together we lived on the Big Island of Hawaii, where we were teachers. Later I became an administrator for the Department of Education. My wife passed on in 2014.

Our four daughters have lives and opportunities that far surpass anything my mother and father could have possibly dreamed about. Lois-Ann is a writer. Kathy works for the U.S. Postal Service. Her twin sister Mona is an elementary school teacher. Carla, who graduated from San Jose State University, has several beauty salons in Northern California.

I am now retired, of course, but I always have something to keep my mind occupied. I enjoy taxidermy, singing, traveling (I have backpacked around the world), golfing, hunting and writing. I have also painted more than 200 paintings, many from my memories of growing up in Kipu.

The last time I visited Kauai was about five years ago. When I was younger, I used to go back to Kauai every year. You always remember your younger days more than anything else.

The entire region of Kipu that encompassed our sugar plantation camp, Hamano Store, Kuraya and Obake ponds and the mile-long, pine-tree lined Kipu Road where the ghost of Felix walked with my father and me, was barely three miles in diameter. But when I was a boy, it was my whole world

Want to read more about Kauai?

www.KauaiStories.net

Made in the USA
Charleston, SC
18 July 2015